RHYTHM REA
FOR DRUMS
Book 2

by GARWOOD WHALEY

International Standard Book Number: 978-1-57463-163-0
Printed and bound in U.S.A.

Copyright © 2010 MEREDITH MUSIC PUBLICATIONS
International Copyright Secured • All Rights Reserved
First Edition
August 2010

No part of this book may be reproduced or transmitted in any form
or by any means, electronic or mechanical, including photocopying,
recording, or by any informational storage or retrieval system
without permission in writing from the publisher.

MEREDITH MUSIC PUBLICATIONS and its stylized double M logo are trademarks
of MEREDITH MUSIC PUBLICATIONS, a division of G.W. Music, Inc.

MEREDITH MUSIC PUBLICATIONS
a division of G.W. Music, Inc.
4899 Lerch Creek Ct., Galesville, MD 20765
http://www.meredithmusic.com

Exclusively Distributed By

HAL•LEONARD CORPORATION
7777 W. BLUEMOUND RD. P.O. BOX 13819 MILWAUKEE, WI 53213

Contents

Introduction..iii

Hand Position...v

Review from Book 1..6

Sixteenth Notes and Rests..8

Flams..14

Cut Time (Alla Breve)...16

Dotted Eighth Notes and Sixteenth Notes..20

Syncopation..24

6/8 Time Signature..28

Eighth Note Triplets...32

Sixteenth Note Triplets..34

Drag..40

Graduation Solo...45

Graduation Duet..46

Technique Builders..47

Advanced Rudiments..48

Introduction

This text provides a systematic approach to reading and understanding rhythm for the beginning-intermediate drummer/percussionist. Intermediate rhythm patterns are introduced on each page in eight-measure studies followed by a short solo. Each solo serves as a page summary and a motivational tool for the student. After all, playing a solo is an important musical accomplishment!

The studies conclude with a *Graduation Solo* and a *Graduation Duet*, both worthy of concert performance. They summarize the material in the book and include many expressive elements. Technique Builders on page forty-seven are exercises designed to develop strength, flexibility and control and should be incorporated into each lesson. The last page is a collection of rudiments that can also be included during lessons. It is not a complete list but serves to develop important techniques and introduce students to a collection of standard rudiments.

Concept

The premise of this publication is to provide a pedagogical template that teachers can use to incorporate their own creative teaching skills. Teachers are encouraged to add dynamics and tempo markings in accordance with each student's individual ability.

What's Included

In addition to rhythm patterns and solos, each page contains something new: dynamics, tempo terms, notation markings, music symbols, and explanations of new rhythms. Music educators and private instructors will find this method to be a comprehensive approach to musical drumming.

COUNTING
- Count all rhythm exercises out loud
- A counting system is included
- Students will develop a system of "rhythm-syllable association"
- They will gain the ability to recall rhythms in new contexts and be able to read rhythms at sight

FOOT TAPPING
- Students should tap their foot on main beats while counting and playing
- Arrows are used to indicate foot taps throughout the book

STICKING
- Two fundamental approaches to sticking: alternate sticking and right-hand lead (left-hand lead if the student is left-handed)
- Alternate sticking: alternating hands with each stroke; **the preferred method for beginning students**
- Right-hand lead: the dominant hand starts each rhythm group. For example, with the rhythmic pattern of two sixteenths and an eight the sticking would be RLR, RLR, RLR

DYNAMICS
- Dynamics are introduced **in text** throughout
- Few dynamics are used in music in order to allow students to focus on rhythm alone

MUSICAL TERMS AND SYMBOLS
- A comprehensive collection of musical terms and symbols appear throughout
- They are included in the music as they are introduced

TIME SIGNATURES
- Only five time signatures are used $\frac{4}{4}$, $\frac{3}{4}$, $\frac{2}{4}$, $\frac{2}{2}$ and $\frac{6}{8}$ so that students can focus on rhythm
- For more advanced study of meters and dynamics use *Primary Handbook for Snare Drum*; ISBN 0-634-02753-0`

TECHNIQUE BUILDERS
- Designed to develop strength, flexibility and control
- Repeat each exercise a minimum of thirty times
- Include them as a regular part of each lesson
- Work slowly and gradually increase speed

RUDIMENTS
- Rudiments are an important "multi-vitamin" for drummers
- They are to drums what scales and arpeggios are to other instrumentalists
- Rudiments from page 48 can be included as a part of each lesson
- Introduce them one at a time as students progress
- Establish the goal of playing all rudiments by the conclusion of this method

Hand Position

There are two snare drum grips: the Matched Grip and the Traditional Grip.

Matched Grip: Both the right and left sticks are held alike when this grip is used. The stick is grasped between the fleshy part of the thumb and the first joint of the index finger (fig. 1). The butt of the stick fits naturally in the main crease of the palm and the remaining three fingers wrap firmly around the stick (fig. 2). Notice that the stick is equally supported by the thumb and index finger (fig. 1) and, the last three fingers (fig. 3). Note carefully the complete grip (fig. 4).

fig. 1

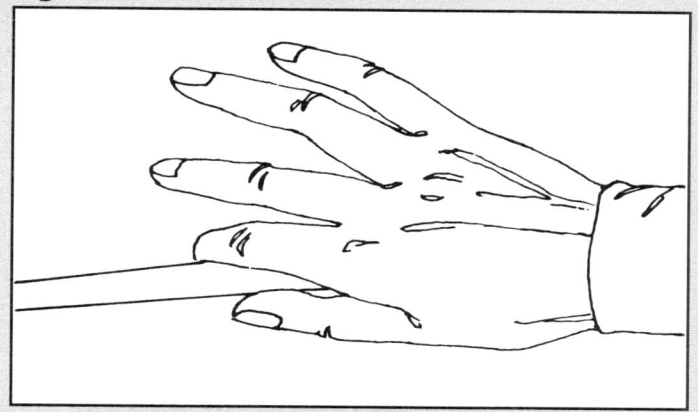

The stick is held between the fleshy part of the thumb and the first joint of the index finger. This provides 50% of the grip

fig. 2

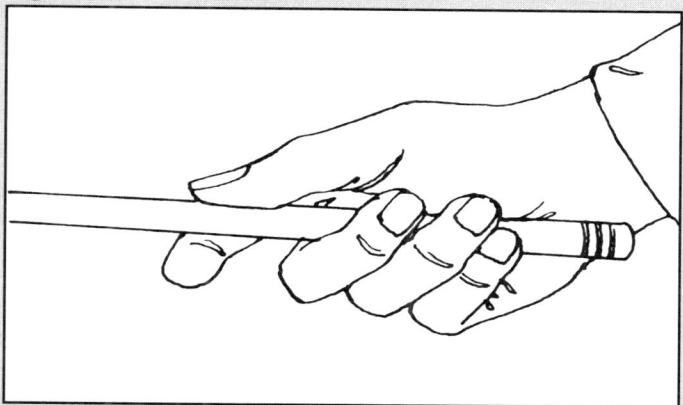

The stick fits naturally in the main crease of the palm. The last three fingers wrap firmly around the stick.

fig. 3

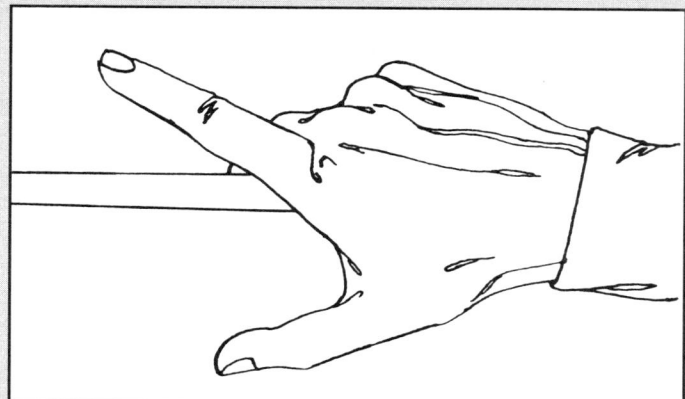

The last three fingers wrap firmly around the stick. This provides 50% of the grip.

fig. 4

The Matched Grip

Traditional Grip: When this grip is utilized, the right hand is held exactly the same as the matched grip. The left hand, however, is quite different. The butt of the stick is grasped in the crotch of the thumb and index finger. The stick rests on the flat of the fourth finger between the first and second joint. The index and third finger lie across the top of the stick. The fifth finger rests beneath the fourth finger. Note that the wrist is curved in toward the body (fig. 5).

Body Position: The drum or practice pad should be at waist level. Both forearms are parallel to the ground. The sticks should form a V on the drum approximately three or four inches from the far rim.

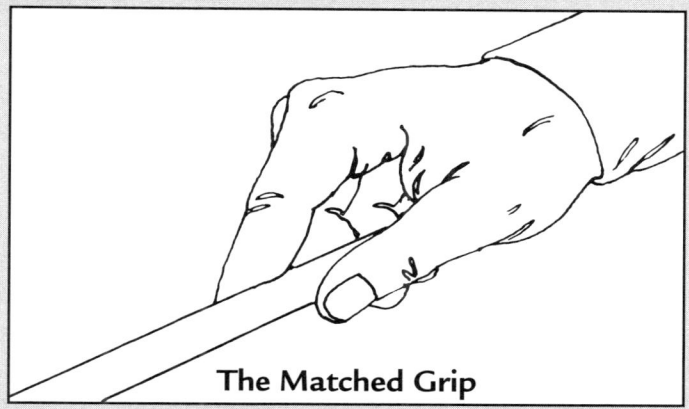

fig. 5

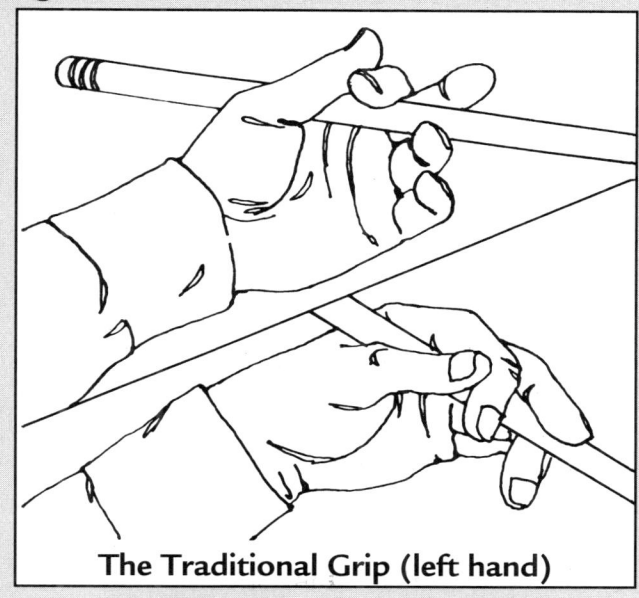

The Traditional Grip (left hand)

REVIEW
Pages 6 and 7 serve as a review of material from *Rhythm Reading for Drums Book 1*. Make sure that you can play these pages before moving on. It is important to master the material on each page.

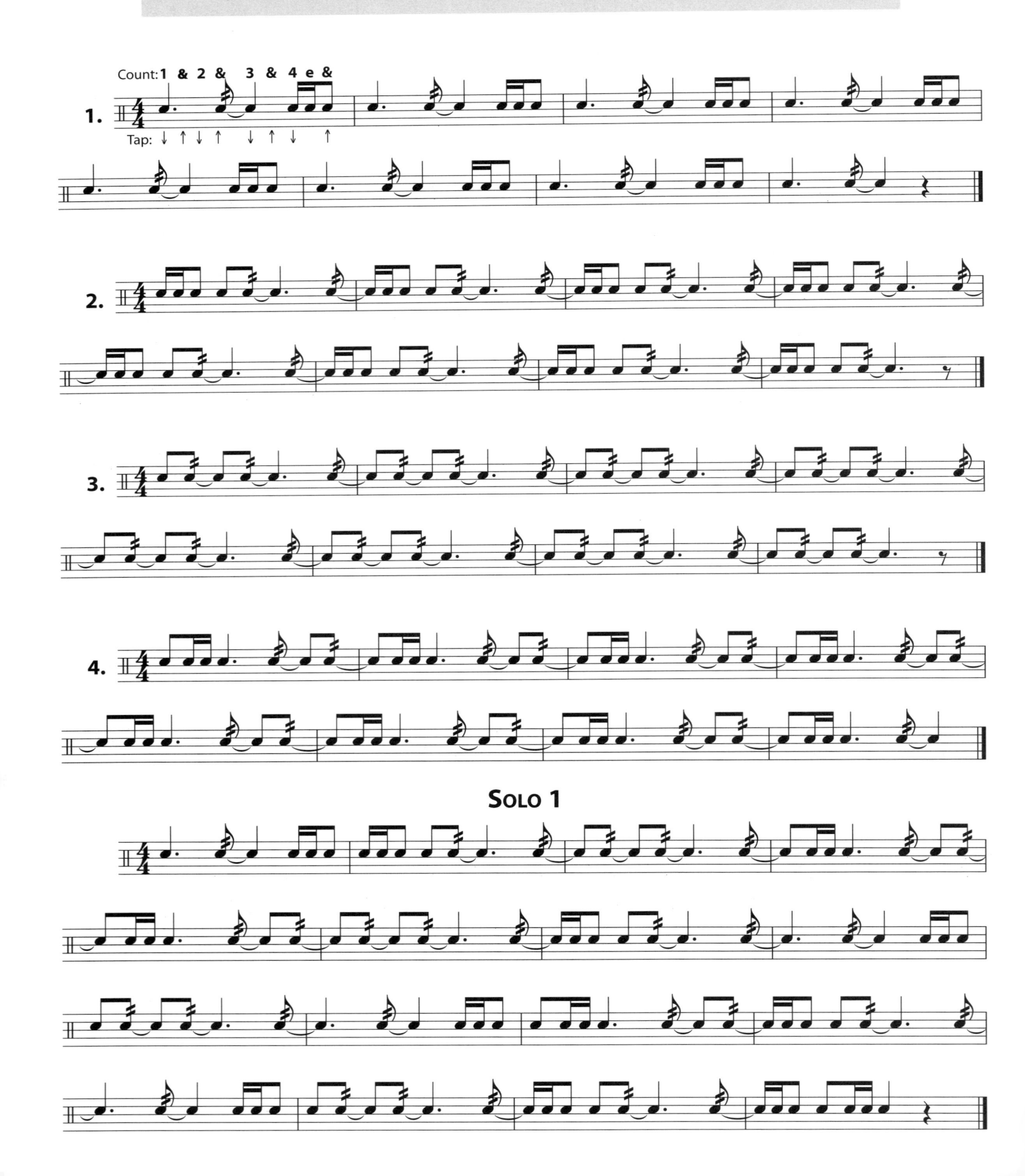

Solo 1

STICK HEIGHT and HAND POSITION

It is important to raise each stick the same height after each stroke. If one hand is raised higher than the other, an uneven sound will occur. Check your hand position often to make sure that not only each stick is raised the same height, but that you are holding the sticks correctly. Good hand position is essential to become a first-class drummer.

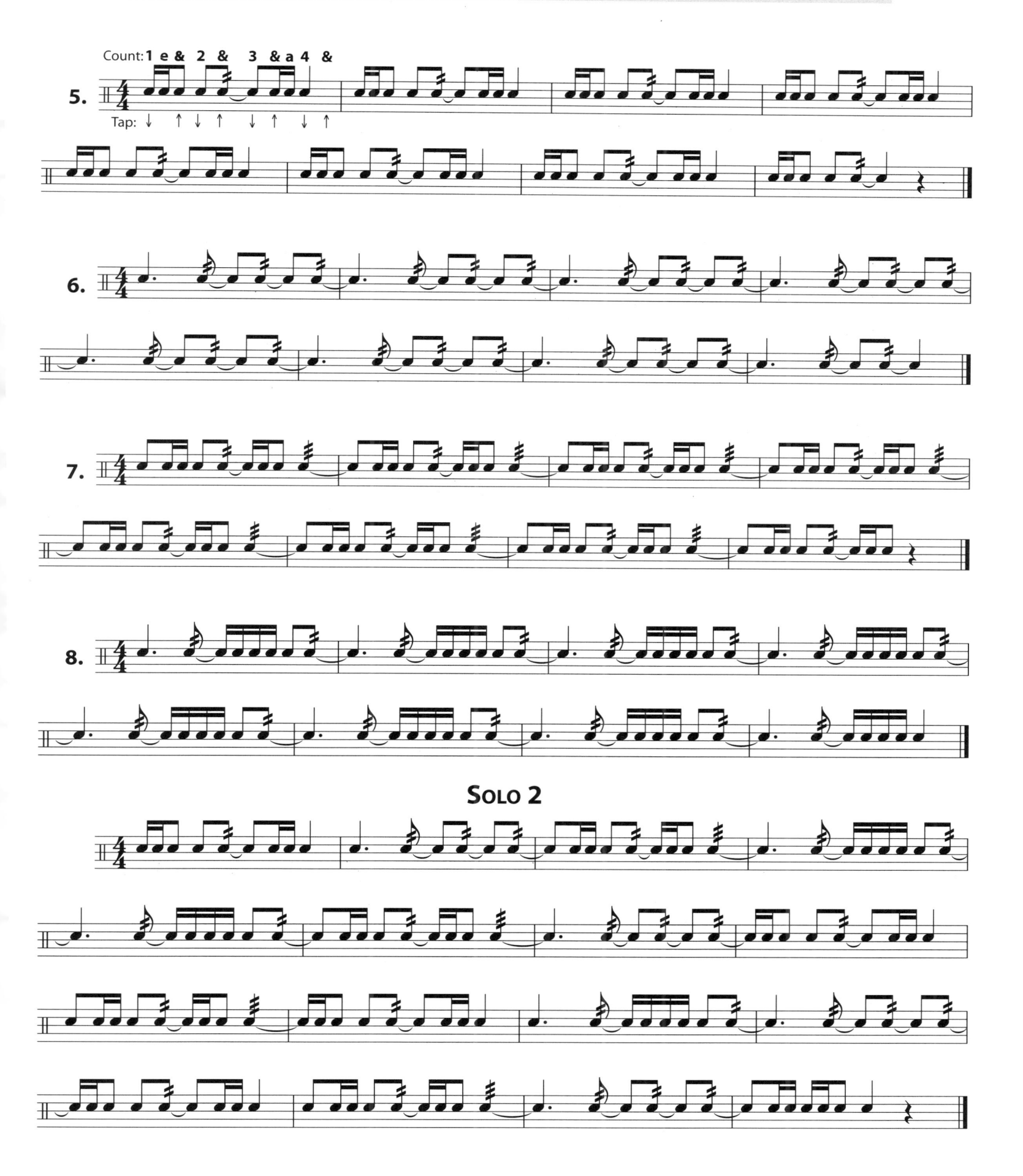

Solo 2

8

SIXTEENTH RESTS 𝄾

A sixteenth rest receives ¼ of the value of a quarter rest or ¼ of a beat. It takes 4 sixteenth rests to fill the space of 1 quarter rest and is notated as follows: 𝄾

SOLO 3

DYNAMICS – A REVIEW
As you know, dynamic marks are used in music to indicate how loud or soft to play.
Here is a review from what you learned in Book 1:
pp - pianissimo (very soft)
p - piano (soft)
mf - mezzo forte (moderately loud)
f - forte (loud)
ff - fortissimo (very loud)

BODY POSITION
As a reminder, the drum or practice pad should be at waist level. Both forearms are parallel to the ground. The sticks should form a V on the drum approximately three or four inches from the far rim.

Count: 1 e & a 2 e & a 3 & 4 &

17.

Tap: ↓ ↑ ↓ ↑ ↓ ↑ ↓ ↑

18.

19.

20.

Solo 5

DYNAMICS – A REVIEW

As you remember the Italian word *Crescendo* means to gradually get louder and the word *Decrescendo* or *Diminuendo* means to gradually get softer. Your teacher may add these dynamic marks to this book to help develop your musical expression.

crescendo = gradually louder

decrescendo or *diminuendo* = gradually softer

SOLO 6

ACCENTS – A REVIEW

Accent marks are added to notes to indicate musical style by emphasizing the note they are placed above. These notes are to be stressed; in other words, played slightly louder than notes without accent marks.

There are two commonly used accents illustrated here:

SOLO 7

RUDIMENTS

Rudiments are to snare drumming what essential foods are to the body! They are exercises to develop technique and control and are also used in rudimental snare drum playing including solos. The rudiments on page 48 are important and should be memorized and practiced slowly, gradually increasing speed.

Count: **1 e & a 2 & 3 e & a**

29.

Tap: ↓ ↑ ↓ ↑ ↓ ↑

30.

31.

32.

Solo 8

FLAMS

A flam combines two notes; a grace note (small note) and a main or primary note. The grace note has no rhythmic value and is played just before the main note. The main note is played on the beat and is louder than the grace note.

SOLO 9

TEMPO MARKINGS (Steady tempo terms)

As you have learned, composers often indicate how slow or fast a piece should be played using either terms (usually in Italian), or a metronome marking. Here are some terms used to indicate a steady tempo:

Largo – very slow; *Grave* – very slow and solemn; *Lento* – slowly

SOLO 10

Lento

TIME SIGNATURE – CUT TIME (alla breve) ¢
A time signature indicating duple meter with the half note rather than the quarter note getting the beat ($\frac{2}{2}$ rather than $\frac{4}{4}$). It can be indicated using either $\frac{2}{2}$ or ¢

Solo 11

SUBITO (sub.)
Subito is the Italian term for quickly or suddenly. It is generally used to indicate a sudden change in dynamics such as: *subito forte* – suddenly change the dynamic to *forte*.

Solo 12

subito f

SIGHT READING
The ability to read a musical work at sight (the first time) is an important and necessary skill for every musician. The best way to develop this skill is to read something new everyday. Select music that is not too difficult and play without stopping (even if you make a mistake!).
To become a good sight reader, you must force yourself to play without stopping to correct mistakes.

49.

50.

51.

52.

Solo 13

DYNAMICS
Here is a new dynamic mark used in music. Again, notated in Italian, the term *mezzo piano* (*mp*) means to play medium soft (between *piano* and *mezzo forte*).

Solo 14

20

> **DOTTED NOTES**
> As you have already learned, a dot following a note adds half of the value of the note or rest that is dotted. A dotted eighth note therefore receives the value of three sixteenth notes. A dotted eight note followed by a sixteenth note is counted as follows:
>
> 1 e & a

57. Count: 1 e & a 2 e & a 3 e & a 4 e & a
Tap: ↓ ↑ ↓ ↑ ↓ ↑ ↓ ↑

58.

59.

60.

Solo 15

TEMPO MARKINGS (Decreasing speed terms)

The Italian term *ritenuto* means to immediately reduce speed.

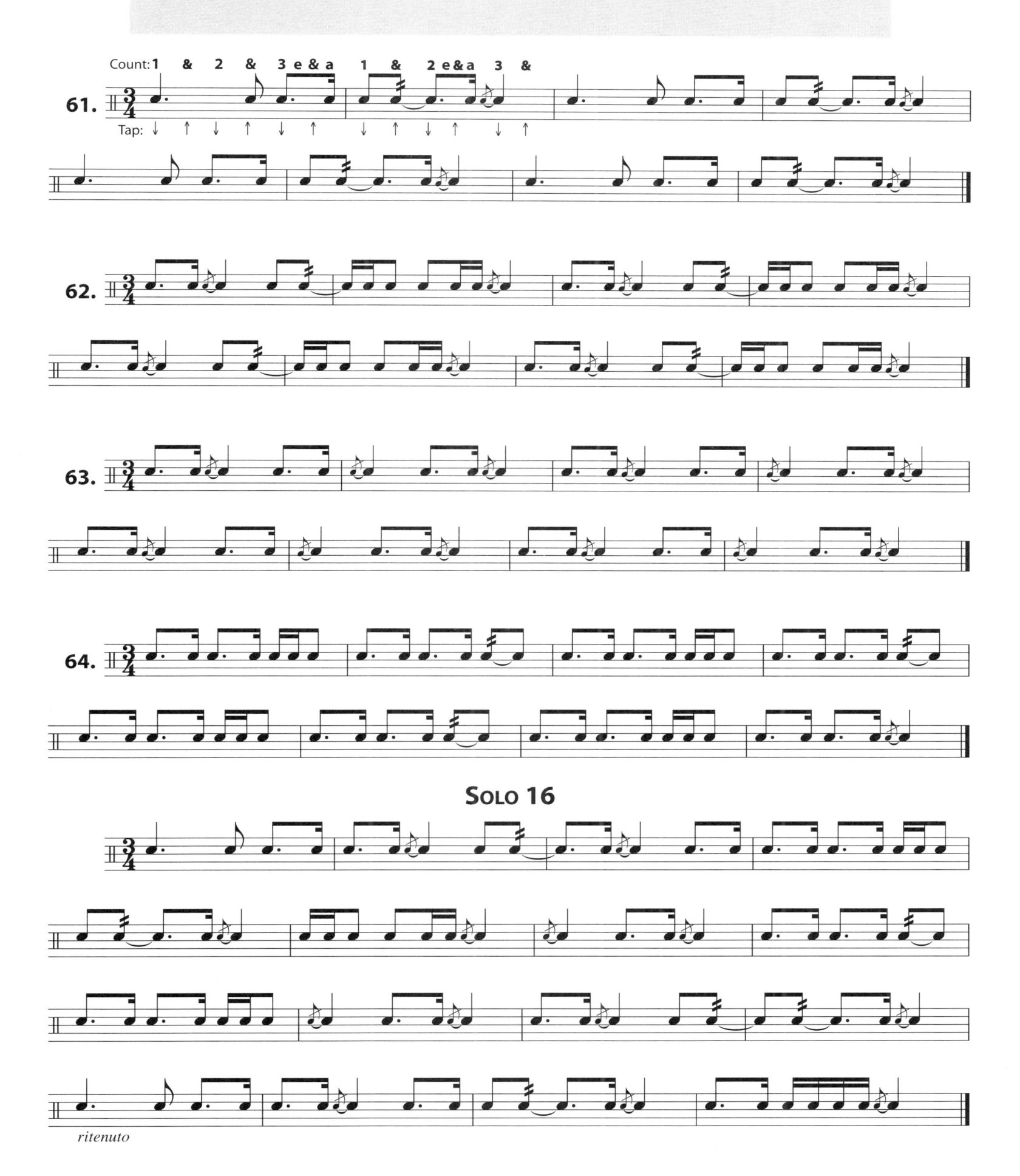

Solo 16

ritenuto

RIM SHOT (Stick Shot)
A rim shot is a special effect produced by striking the rim and the drum head at the same time. It is a loud accented sound. A stick shot is a similar effect produced by holding one stick on the drum head and striking that stick with the other. It also produces a loud accented sound. Note the stick shots in the solo below marked with an ✖ note head.

Solo 17

MOLTO

The Italian term *molto* means "much" – like *molto marcato* (very *marcato-accented*)

molto marcato

SYNCOPATION

Syncopation is the stressing of weak beats over notes that are normally strong beats. In 4/4 time, beats 1 and 3 are generally the strong beats. With syncopation, beats 2 and 4 would be stressed thus providing an "off-beat" feeling. This "off-beat" feel is often found in jazz and popular music.

Count: 1 & 2 & 3 & 4 & 1 & 2 & 3 & 4 &

73.

Tap: ↓ ↑ ↓ ↑ ↓ ↑ ↓ ↑ ↓ ↑ ↓ ↑ ↓ ↑ ↓ ↑

74.

75.

76.

Solo 19

25

DYNAMICS
Here is a new dynamic mark used in music. Again, notated in Italian, the term *più fortissimo* or *fortississimo* (*fff*) means to play very, very loud.

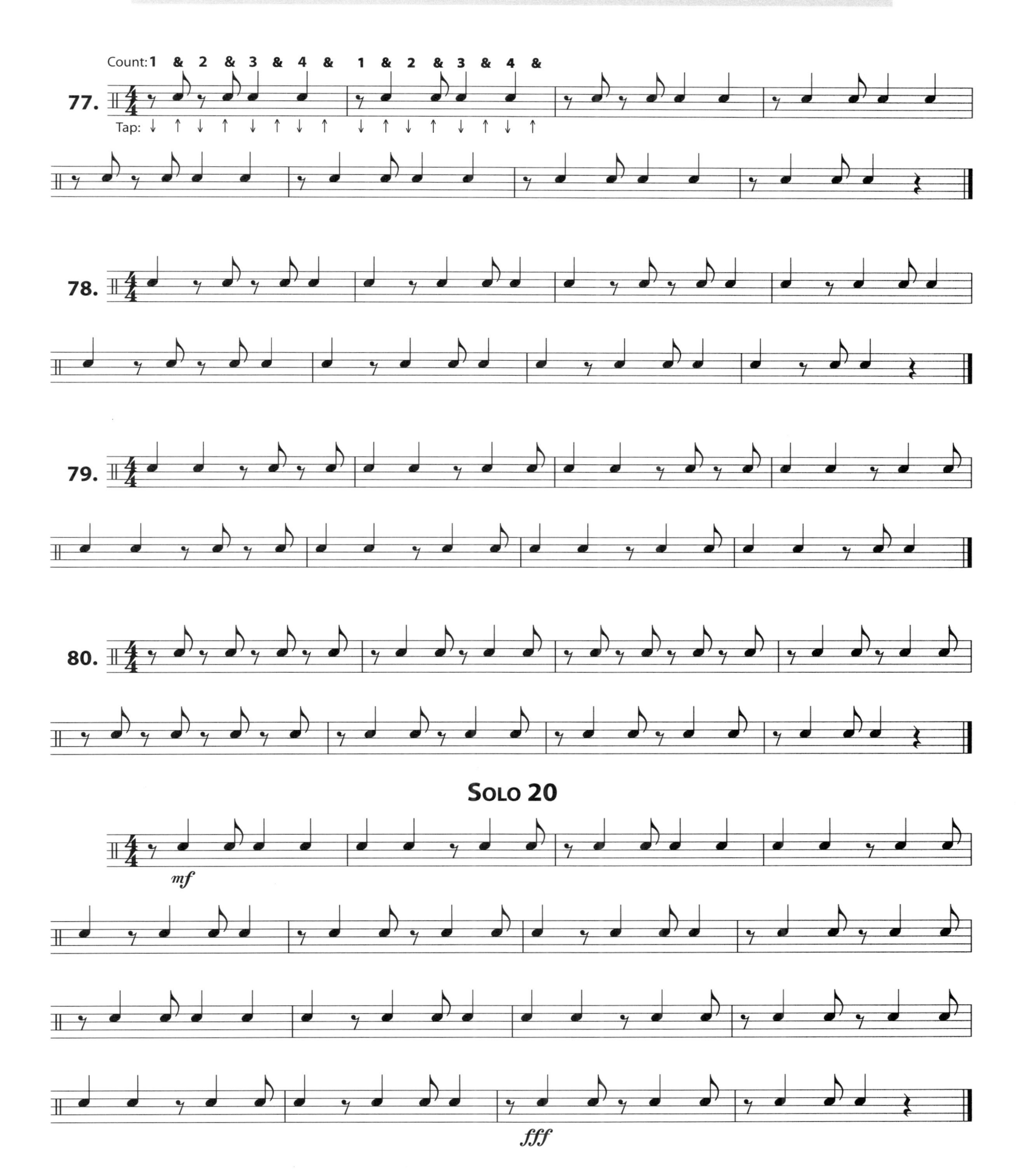

Solo 20

mf

fff

MAESTOSO

The Italian term *maestoso* is a stylistic term meaning majestically – to play the passage marked *maestoso* in a majestic manner.

Solo 21

TIED NOTES
When a curved line connects two notes of the same pitch (as in snare drum notation), play one note for the combined counts of the tied notes. In #85 below, the second measure sounds like the first measure (the second of the two tied notes is not struck).

Solo 22

TIME SIGNATURE (6/8)

6/8 time can be played ("felt") in 6 beats per measure (slower music) or 2 beats per measure (faster music). It is often played with a slight pulse on beats 1 and 4 of each measure.

89. Count: 1 2 3 **4** 5 6 | **1** 2 3 **4** 5 6
Tap: ↓   ↓   ↓   ↓

90.

91.

92.

Solo 23

MARCHES in 6/8

Many marches are written in 6/8 time. The well-known marches of John Philip Sousa like *Semper Fidelis*, *The Washington Post*, *The Liberty Bell* and *El Capitan* are all written in 6/8 time.

Count: **1** 2 3 **4** 5 6 **1** 2 3 **4** 5 6

93.

Tap: ↓ ↓ ↓ ↓

94.

95.

96.

SOLO 24

TEMPO MARKINGS (Steady tempo terms)
Here are some additional terms used to indicate a steady tempo:
Vivace – vivacious, fast;
Presto – very fast.

97. Count: 1 2 3 **4** 5 6 **1** 2 3 **4** 5 6
    Tap: ↓ ↓ ↓ ↓

98.

99.

100.

Solo 25

Vivace

31

MENO
The Italian term *meno* means less as in *meno forte* – a little softer than *forte*.

SOLO 26

f

meno f

EIGHTH-NOTE TRIPLETS
Eighth-note triplets are a group of three evenly spaced eighth notes played in the space of two eighth notes. There are several methods for counting them including:
1 trip-let **2** trip-let, **1** la lee **2** la lee and the method used here **1** & a **2** & a.

105.

106.

107.

108.

Solo 27

DYNAMICS

Here is a new dynamic mark used in music. Again, notated in Italian, the term *più pianissimo* or *pianississimo* (***ppp***) means to play very, very soft.

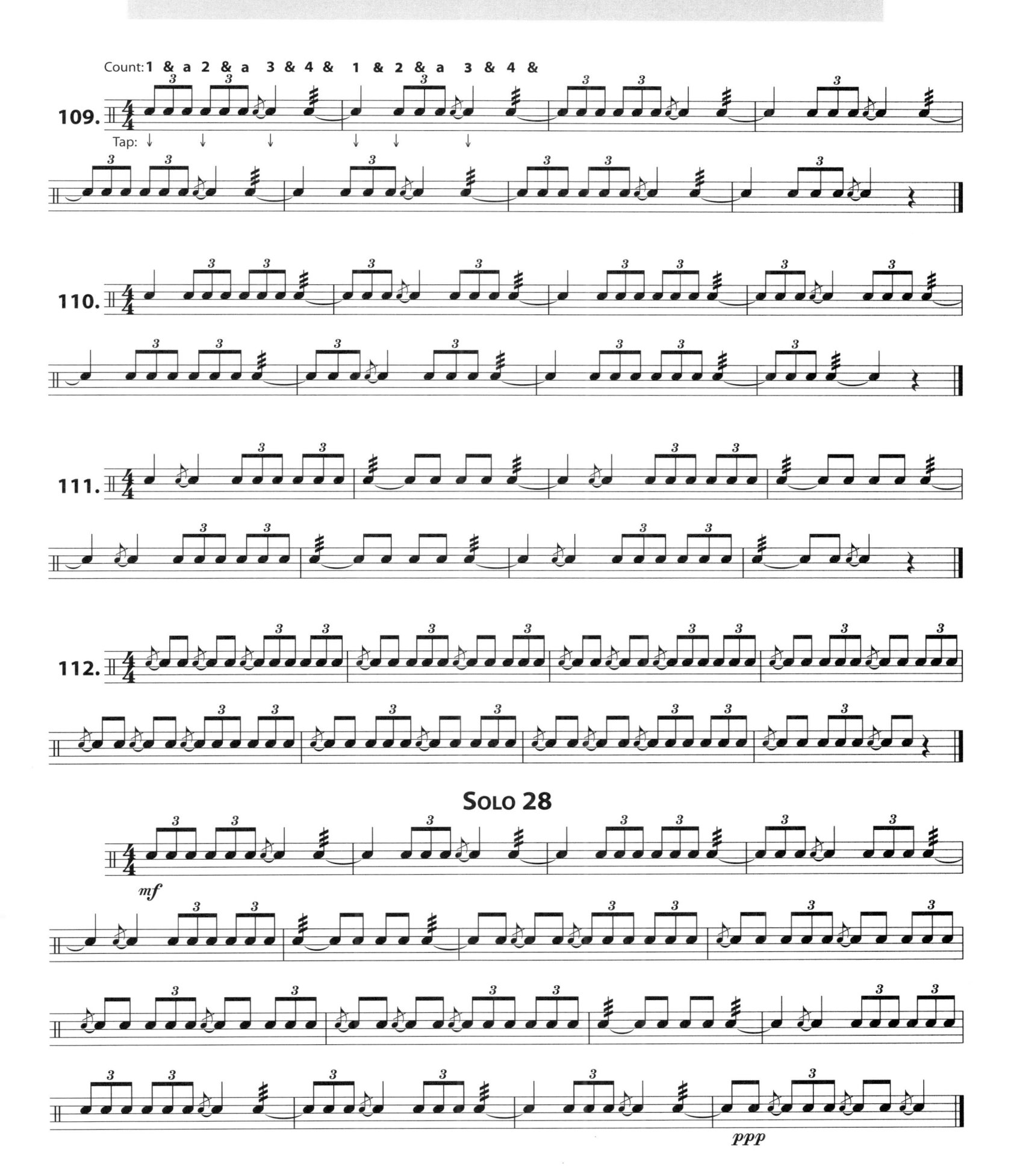

SIXTEENTH-NOTE TRIPLETS

Sixteenth-note triplets are a group of three evenly spaced sixteenth notes played in the space of two sixteenth notes. Since these notes are usually played quickly, it is difficult to count each note. Therefore, it is advisable to simply count the note on which the triplet begins either on the beat using the beat number or on & using that syllable.

Solo 29

TEMPO MARKINGS (Decreasing speed terms)
The Italian term *allargando* (*allarg.*) means to get gradually slower and broader.

allargando

TEMPO MARKINGS (Increasing speed terms)
The Italian term *stringendo* (*string.*) means to get gradually faster, usually with a crescendo.

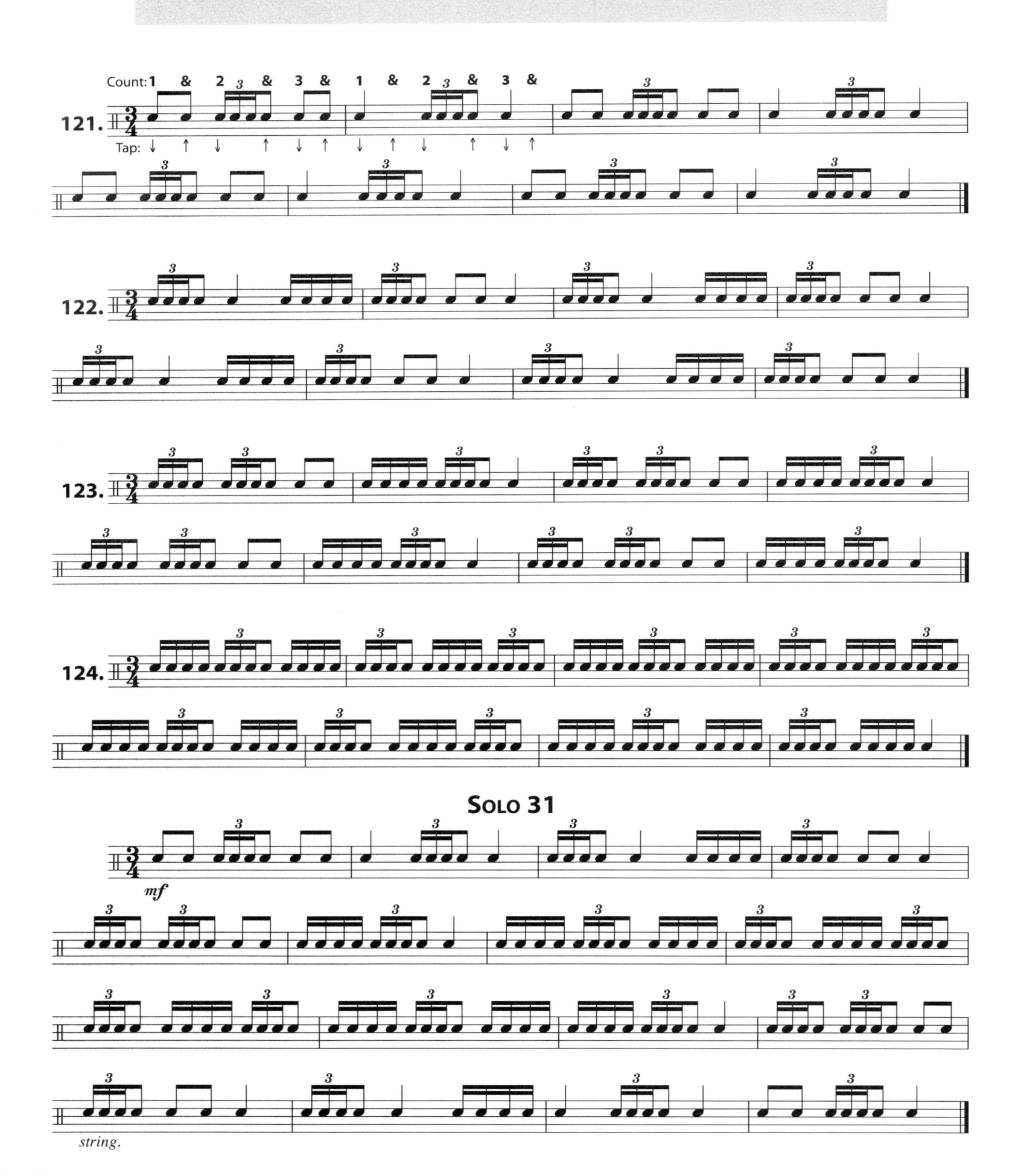

121.

122.

123.

124.

Solo 31

mf

string.

forte-piano (*fp*)

The Italian term *forte-piano* (*fp*) means to play loud and immediately soft.

Solo 32

RUBATO
The Italian term *rubato* means to be flexible with the tempo. Create this effect by alternating slight *accelerandi* and *ritardandi* for expression.

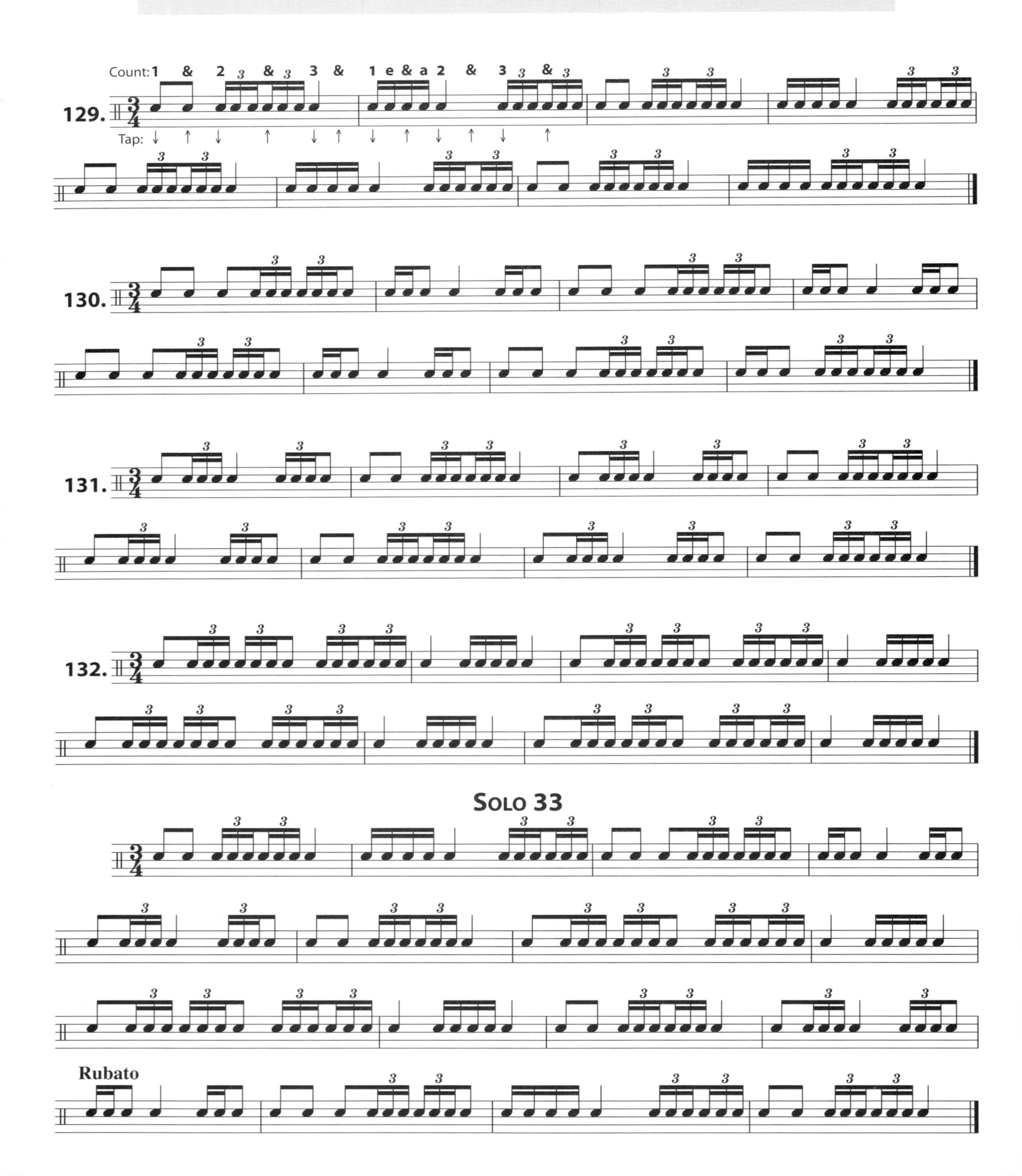

Solo 33

Rubato

TEMPO MARKINGS

L'istesso tempo simply means to keep the same tempo.

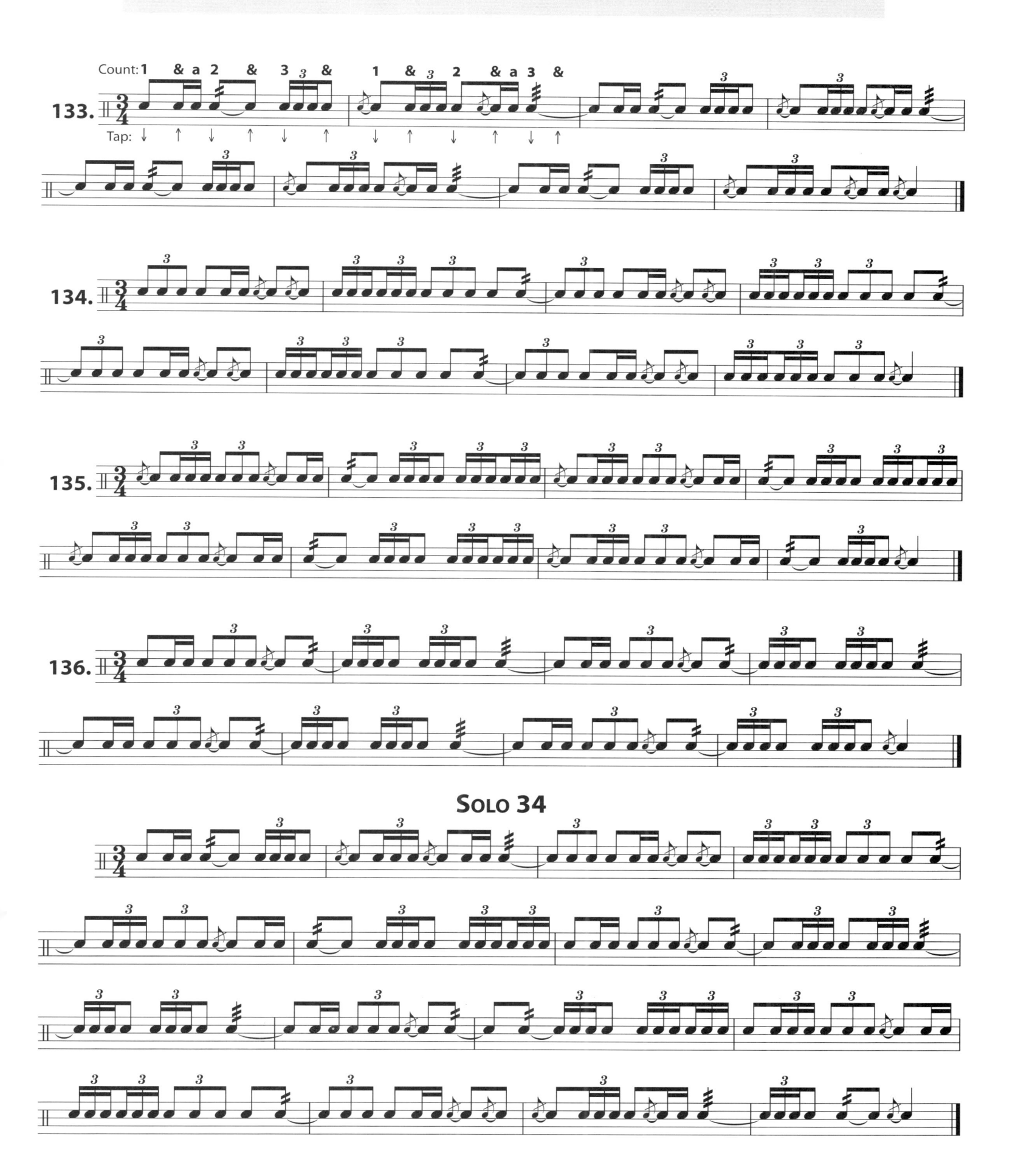

Solo 34

DRAG

A drag combines three notes; two grace notes (small notes) and a main or primary note. The grace notes have no rhythmic value and are played just before the main note. The main note is played on the beat and is louder than the grace notes. It is played with a double bounce and a single stroke.

SOLO 35

Sforzando (*sfz* or *sf*)
The Italian term *sforzando* means to play a sudden, strong accent.

Solo 36

MORENDO
The Italian term *morendo* means gradually softer and dying away.

Solo 37

morendo

Rinforzanodo (*rf*, *rfz* or *rinf.*)
The Italian term *rinforzando* means to play a very strong accent, similar to *sforzando*.

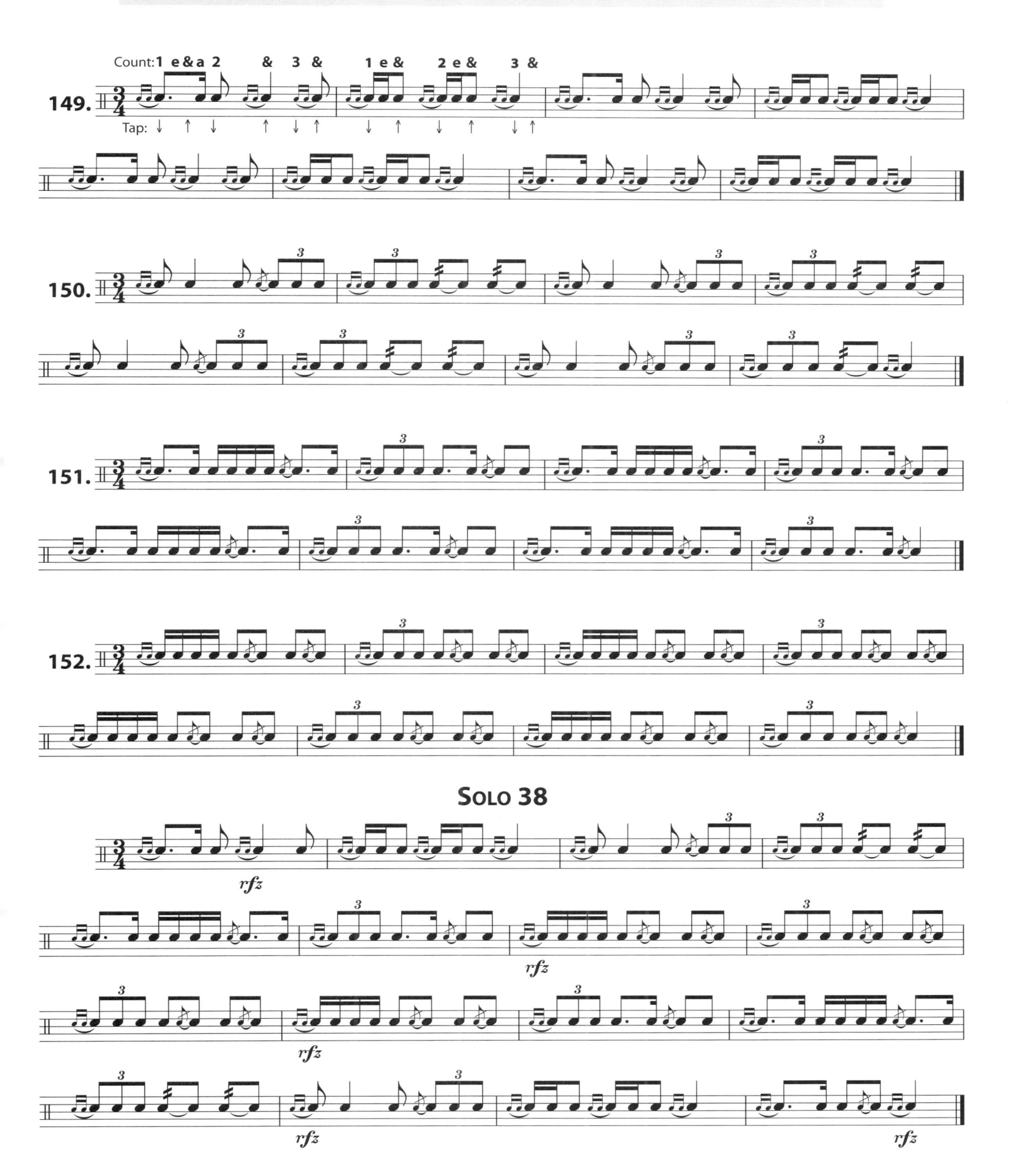

Solo 38

TEMPO MARKINGS

The Italian term *tempo primo* (**Tempo I**) means to return to the original (first) tempo of the piece.

Solo 39

allargando

Tempo I

GRADUATION SOLO

Congratulations! You have successfully completed this book and mastered the many rhythmic challenges contained within it. You have also learned many terms, symbols and musical expressions that will help you to become an outstanding musician. Throughout this book you have been introduced to musical terms and dynamics that are included in the *Graduation Solo*. Play them carefully in order to produce a musically expressive performance.

GRADUATION DUET

Duets are an excellent ensemble builder; the ability to play an independent part with another musician. This is a necessary skill for playing in a group such as band or orchestra. Prepare each part of the duet and perform it with your teacher or another student. It will be a fun piece to play during a concert.

TECHNIQUE BUILDERS

The exercises below are designed to develop strength, flexibility and control. To achieve the optimum benefit, each exercise must be repeated a minimum of thirty times a day. Work slowly and gradually increase speed.

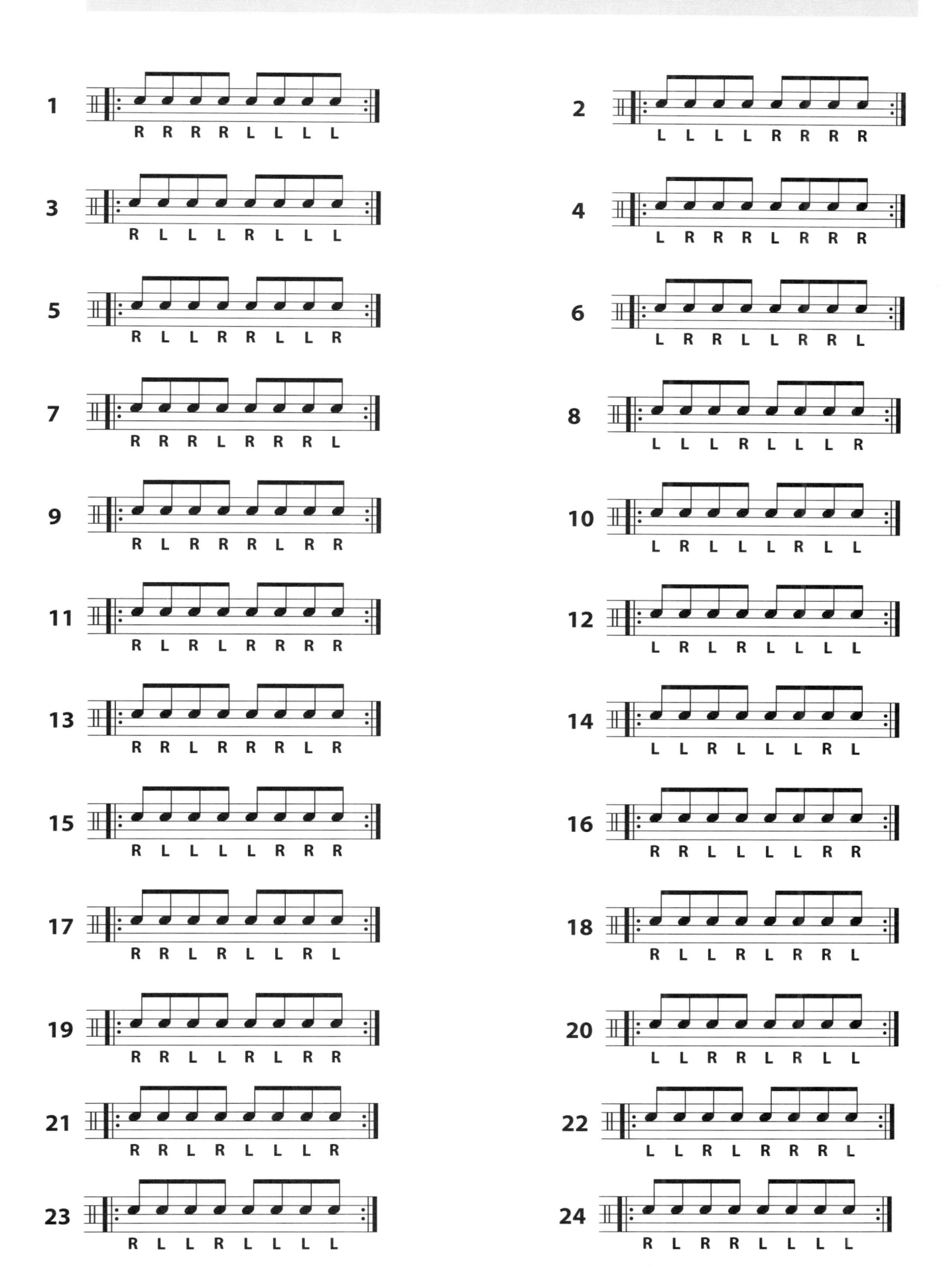

1. R R R R L L L L
2. L L L L R R R R
3. R L L L R L L L
4. L R R R L R R R
5. R L L R R L L R
6. L R R L L R R L
7. R R R L R R R L
8. L L L R L L L R
9. R L R R R L R R
10. L R L L L R L L
11. R L R L R R R R
12. L R L R L L L L
13. R R L R R R L R
14. L L R L L L R L
15. R L L L L R R R
16. R R L L L L R R
17. R R L R L L R L
18. R L L R L R R L
19. R R L L R L R R
20. L L R R L R L L
21. R R L R L L L R
22. L L R L R R R L
23. R L L R L L L L
24. R L R R L L L L

ADVANCED RUDIMENTS

Rudiments are to snare drumming what essential foods are to the body! They are exercises to develop technique and control and are also used in rudimental snare drum playing including solos. The rudiments below are important and should be memorized and practiced slowly, gradually increasing speed.

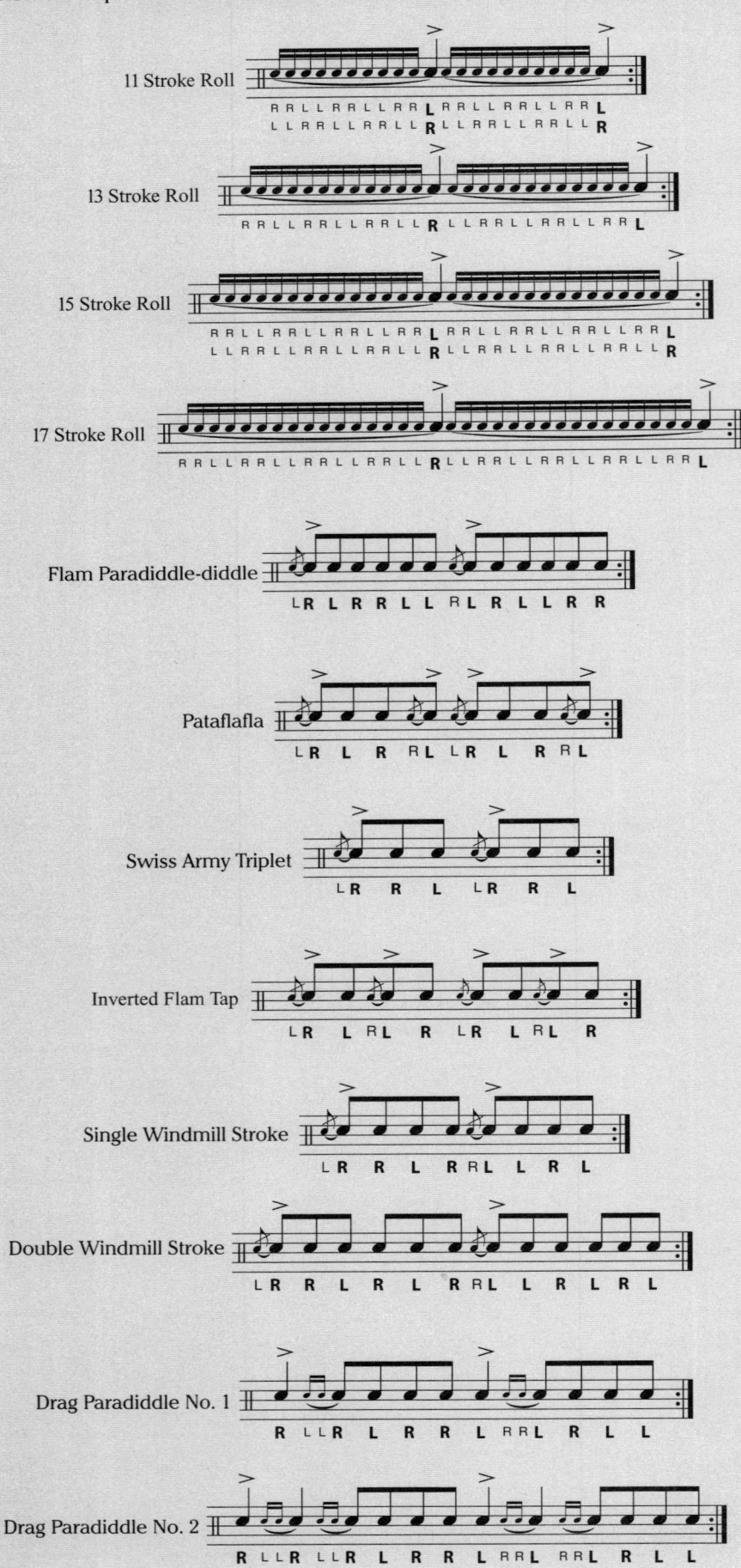

11 Stroke Roll
RRLLRRLLRR**L** RRLLRRLLRR**L**
LLRRLLRRLL**R** LLRRLLRRLL**R**

13 Stroke Roll
RRLLRRLLRRLL**R** LLRRLLRRLLRR**L**

15 Stroke Roll
RRLLRRLLRRLLRR**L** RRLLRRLLRRLLRR**L**
LLRRLLRRLLRRLL**R** LLRRLLRRLLRRLL**R**

17 Stroke Roll
RRLLRRLLRRLLRRLL**R** LLRRLLRRLLRRLLRR**L**

Flam Paradiddle-diddle
L R L R R L L R L R L L R R

Pataflafla
L R L R R L L R L R R L

Swiss Army Triplet
L R R L L R R L

Inverted Flam Tap
L R L R L R L R L R L R

Single Windmill Stroke
L R R L R R L L R L

Double Windmill Stroke
L R R L R L R R L L R L R L

Drag Paradiddle No. 1
R LL R L R R L RR L R L L

Drag Paradiddle No. 2
R LL R LL R L R R L RR L RR L R L L